Cat Album No. 3

PLAYFUL KITTENS

Photos by
Nobuo Honda

Heian

Other books by Nobuo Honda:

Exploring Kittens
Exploring Kittens II
Five Kittens
Cat Album Series

1. Kitten Dreams
2. Catnaps
3. Playful Kittens
4. Houseful of Kittens

All published by Heian International, Inc.
Also published in England, France, Germany,
and Japan

Photos by Nobuo Honda

First Edition: 1985

Heian International, Inc.
P.O. Box 1013
Union City, California 94587

ISBN: 0-89346-255-1
Printed in Japan

19

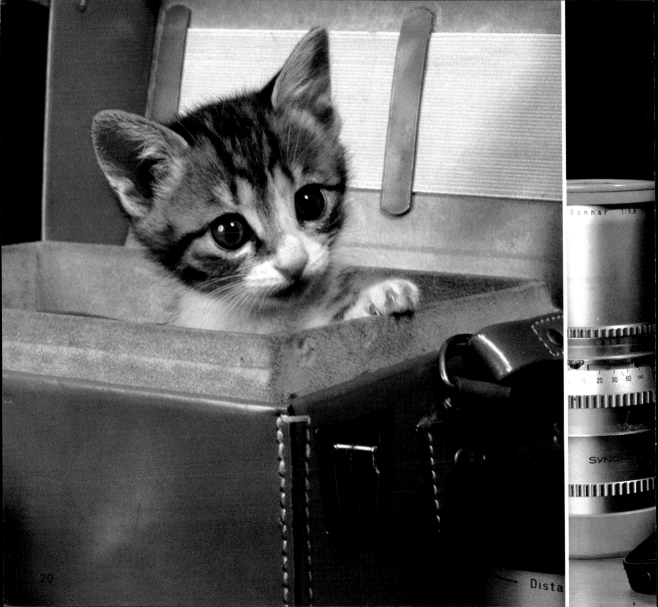